"Jesus Rode a Donkey gives us an alternative to the current culture war that divides America and its faith communities. I can't think of a better Election Day gift for my Republican—and Democratic—friends.

—William McKinney, Ph.D., President,
Pacific School of Religion

"You do not have to be a Republican to be a good Christian. Dr. Seger's excellent book helps make it clear that there are several strategic Biblical issues in America in 2006 that are better addressed by Democrats. In the bright light of Scripture, many of us evangelicals, committed to its authority, truly dislike the forced dilemma between being a grieving Democrat or a frustrated Republican. Perhaps, as Dr. Seger reminds us, Jesus rode a donkey once, and his commands may become more clearly seen in the choices the present donkey makes for our future. Engaging some of the divine wisdom of this book could help make that happen."

—Paul de Vries, Ph.D., President,
New York Divinity School

"Linda Seger shows us a Christianity that overcomes divisions of liberal and conservative. But she also makes clear how liberal values are deeply rooted in the gospel message. Liberals need not think that their values are somehow less religious or Biblical than those of conservative Republicans. Seger does trenchant analyses of the conflicting values underlying conservative and liberal policy choices and asks which are closer to the values of Jesus, values rooted in love, compassion, and justice. This is an important book for this time in American life."

—Rosemary Radford Ruether, Ph.D., Professor of Theology,
Claremont Graduate University and Claremont School of Theology, and author of
Sexism and God-Talk and Integrating Ecofeminism, Globalization, and World Religions

"As a Baptist preacher's kid, Christian, and the only Democrat from El Paso County (an epicenter of Religious Right organizations), I am frequently compelled to point out the hypocrisy of Republican "value based" legislation. Linda Seger's book Jesus Rode a Donkey has given me reams of quotes, and I have used up at least one highlighter while reading it. It has also provided me with a strong defense against those who have at times called me "devil worshiper," "sinner," "evil," and—worst of all—a Democrat!"

—Michael Merrifield, State Representative,
District 18, El Paso County, Colorado State Legislature

"*Jesus Rode a Donkey* aptly demonstrates that no one secular political party has a lock on religious and Biblical authenticity and application. Those who are interested in this timely topic will admire Seger's effort to bring clarity and balance to American religious and political interaction."

—**William Durland, Ph.D.,**
author of *God or Nations: Radical Theology for the Religious Peace Movement*

"In this thoughtful book about crucial issues facing Americans today, Linda Seger calls for a new public discourse. Her perspective as a born-again Christian and a liberal Democrat challenges the right-wing stereotype that persons of deep faith are, or should be, conservative Republicans. *Jesus Rode a Donkey* also challenges left-wing Americans, especially liberal Christians, to affirm the vital connections between their personal faith and public policy."

— **Lloyd E. Ambrosius, Ph.D., Samuel Clark Waugh**
Distinguished Professor of International Relations and
Professor of History, University of Nebraska

"In a time when cultural awareness has become a requirement for effective global engagement, and a critical element in efforts to combat the growing threat of terrorism, Linda Seger offers a thoughtful treatise on tolerance and understanding among diverse religious traditions. While her book focuses on Christianity in the modern American political context, her approach is useful to anyone seeking understanding of different religions, customs, and cultural traditions."

—**Colonel Thomas Dempsey, U.S. Army (Retired),**
a regional studies specialist with experience in
conflict resolution in both the Middle East and Africa

"In *Jesus Rode a Donkey*, Dr. Linda Seger has taken on today's "story" of controversial partisan politics, government and religion, and the sensitive issues facing contemporary Christianity. Supported with excellent research and Biblical references, Seger provides us with a unique and fascinating critique of what it means to be a devoted follower of Christianity in America from a more liberal point of view."

—**Kate McCallum, writer, media producer, and**
founder of the Center for Conscious Creativity

"Linda Seger's book is an eloquent breath of fresh air in the political debate. *Jesus Rode a Donkey* is a clarion call for comity and peace-seeking dialogue. This book provides a well-marked path for those interested in removing the rancor and toxicity from our political discourse. In a rational world, every American President and Cabinet Secretary would be compelled to read it."

—**Robert Grant, award-winning movie producer and writer**

JESUS RODE A DONKEY

Why Republicans Don't Have the Corner on Christ

Linda Seger, Th.D.

ADAMS MEDIA
AVON, MASSACHUSETTS

Published by Adams Media, an F+W Publications Company
57 Littlefield Street
Avon, MA 02322
www.adamsmedia.com

ISBN: 1-59337-619-7

Printed in the United States of America.

J I H G F E D C B A

Library of Congress Cataloging in Publication Data
Seger, Linda.
Jesus rode a donkey / by Linda Seger.
p.   cm.
Includes bibliographical references and index.
ISBN 1-59337-619-7
1. Christians—United States—Political activity. 2. Christianity and politics—
United States. 3. Democratic Party (U.S.) I. Title.
BR526.S44 2006
261.70973—dc22
2006005208

This publication is designed to provide accurate and authoritative information with regard to the subject matter covered. It is sold with the understanding that the publisher is not engaged in rendering legal, accounting, or other professional advice. If legal advice or other expert assistance is required, the services of a competent professional person should be sought.

—From a *Declaration of Principles* jointly adopted by a Committee of the American Bar Association and a Committee of Publishers and Associations

Many of the designations used by manufacturers and sellers to distinguish their products are claimed as trademarks. Where those designations appear in this book and Adams Media was aware of a trademark claim, the designations have been printed with initial capital letters.

Unless otherwise noted, the Bible used as a source is the *New Jerusalem Bible*, Doubleday & Company (1973).

This book is available at quantity discounts for bulk purchases.
For information, please call 1-800-872-5627.

*Dedicated to my uncle, Dr. Norman Graebner,
who has taught American history and American diplomacy
for more than sixty years. His dedication to democracy,
and his dignity and grace, have been a model to me all my life.*

*To my researcher, Sue Terry, who knows where to find
everything—fast. I thank her for her generosity, care, and
spirituality. Without her, I could not have written his book.*

Contents

>⋅⊢◆〉⋅○⋅〈◆⊢⋅≺

>–I–‹›–O–‹›–I–≺

Acknowledgments

In all my books, I ask readers to give me feedback before I send the book to the publisher. I have been particularly thankful to this group of readers. Thank you to my uncle, Dr. Norman Graebner, for adding quotes, giving me books, and checking facts for me. Thanks also:

- To my Quaker friend, Dr. Bill Durland, Ph.D. in politics and religion, who has guided me through several chapters; to my neighbor Tom Radcliffe, who has worked in the White House under several administrations and helped with the chapter titled "Secrets, Lies, and Deceptions"; and to William Flavin from the U.S. Army War College, who provided me with many papers and fact checks in the "War and Peace" chapter.
- To my fellow Christian Democrat readers, who gave me copious notes and wonderful insights: Pamela Jaye Smith, Kim Peterson, Cathleen Loeser, Bobbie Sue Nave, and Jim Nave.

- To my Christian Republican readers, who were so generous with their time, their insights, and their ideas about how to make this a book that Republicans would also like to read; in particular, thanks to Debra Weitala, from South Dakota, who read every chapter and kept me on track, answered many e-mail questions, and so lovingly proved how beautifully Republicans and Democrats can work together. And thanks to my Republican neighbor Steve Berendt for our ten-hour day filled with stimulating discussions of ideas and with his brilliant suggestions for honing the language of the book.
- To Dr. Cheri Junk for help with Chapters 1 and 2.
- To Kristin Howard for her help with Chapter 1.
- To Tirtza and Abe Weschler for help on Chapter 3.
- To Ann Grant Martin and Pam Jones for their comments on Chapter 6.
- To Devorah Cutler-Rubinstein for help with Chapters 7 and 8.

Many thanks to my researcher, Sue Terry, to whom this book is dedicated. I thank her for her brilliance, generosity, and support, and for always being there when I needed her.

Thanks to my agent, Janet Benrey, and thanks to the many people at Adams Media who have worked on this book. In particular, thanks to my editor, Paula Munier; development editor Larry Shea; copyeditor Kate Petrella; and book designers Paul Beatrice and Colleen Cunningham.

Many thanks to my assistant, Sarah Callbeck, for always being there when needed, for keeping her good humor and kind presence, and for being willing to deal with the many tedious details necessary. And for never letting me down! And to Martha Callbeck, for her good help on footnoting the chapters.

And thanks always to my husband, Peter Hazen Le Var, for reading chapters and for continuing to love me despite knowing what life is like when I'm writing a book!

Note: In order to be inclusive, my Biblical quotes come from the *New Jerusalem Bible*, which is used by Catholics and Protestants alike. Very occasionally, another translation is used.

Introduction

If you think about it—no one has a corner on God. Not Republicans or Democrats, men or women, black or white, Asian, Hispanic; nor any culture, nationality, or religious sect. If those of us who are Christians understand anything about the nature of Christ, we know he was a man for all seasons, a Son of God for all ages.

And yet, leading up to the election of 2004 and in the months following, I kept hearing about the Republican "values" vote as the "Christian vote." Supposedly, George W. Bush had the Christian vote, and those of us who were Democrats and Christians were not in line with core Christian values.

As someone who has always been religious, I became increasingly distressed by the growing divisions among Christians. I grew up Lutheran, the granddaughter of a Missouri Synod Lutheran minister. My mother was Lutheran, and my father was Presbyterian. It was not unusual for me to join my father to sing in the choir or to attend a Methodist church, because I liked their nonliturgical service. I became a born-again Christian my last year at Colorado College in Colorado Springs, helped in my own personal spiritual search by the evangelical Christian group, the Navigators, as well as by a Bible church located nearby. My first teaching job was at Grand Canyon College, a Southern Baptist college in Phoenix. Later, I taught at two Church of the Brethren colleges—McPherson College and University of La Verne.

I attended the Graduate Theological Union seminary in Berkeley, California, which is a consortium that includes Baptist, Lutheran, Episcopal, Presbyterian, and Catholic seminaries. My seminary, Pacific School of Religion, prepares ministers in both the Methodist and United Church of Christ. While there, I received an M.A. and a Th.D. One summer I did the Ignatian Exercises, which are the Jesuit exercises, usually done for five weeks by those entering the priesthood, but occasionally done by laypeople. These exercises included Bible reading, prayer, and meditating three hours a day on the life of Christ. This practice changed my life on many profound levels.

Throughout these years, I attended many different churches—Evangelical churches, Episcopal, Catholic, Methodist, Presbyterian, Lutheran, Baptist—but it took me some years to find my church home. One day in Phoenix in 1969, I decided to attend a Quaker Meeting (Society of Friends). I walked in, sat down, and knew I was home.

In 1993 I returned to graduate school to study feminist liberation theology. Although I recognize that anything with the "F" word is a red flag to some, I found that my studies brought me more deeply in touch with the liberating work of Christ. Much of my study previously had been in Biblical studies, church history, religion and the arts, and Christian mysticism, but I felt I had not brought my religion sufficiently into the social and political world. I did my internship with a Catholic charity in the Philippines (the Women's Economic Development and Earth Foundation—WODEEF). My time there changed my life, and the people I met and the work of WODEEF deeply touched me.

On the political level, I have also met the best of both conservatives and liberals. I come from an extended family that includes conservatives, fundamentalists, radicals, liberals, and mainstream Christians and find that we are all able to get along.

I grew up in a Republican household, although my mother switched to voting Democrat during the Vietnam War. My father was a staunch conservative—he liked things the way they were, and was a grounded, stable, and very kind man. He saw no need for change since he believed that our little town of Peshtigo, Wisconsin, was the center of the universe. He was content to go to his drugstore every morning, filling prescriptions for the 2,500 people from our town, most of whom he knew. He didn't confront. He didn't make waves. He played it safe, never took risks, never questioned. He didn't take stands, even when, at times, it seemed important to stand up and be counted. Yet, he was never hateful, never would willingly hurt anyone, and was one of the most generous people I've ever known.

My mother was a liberal in outlook. She was curious about the world around her and the world outside the boundaries of Peshtigo, of Wisconsin, and of the United States. She believed in possibilities, potential, imagination, what might be. She was willing to analyze and ask the Big Questions—about people, about values, about our lives. She was a problem-solver. If there was a way to make things better, she was willing to give it a try. She taught me to question and analyze and envision something better. Before I went to college, she told me, "It's all right to question your religion. If your religion can't hold up to questioning, it's not much good anyway." She believed Christianity was strong enough for any of my little but important questions, and by questioning, my faith would become stronger. She helped us understand that nurturing our potential and nurturing the potential of others was a worthy goal to make the world better. She wasn't afraid of change, but embraced it—and found the adventure of new experiences, new approaches, and creative ways to solve problems exhilarating.

I took after my mother. My sister took after my father.

I have seen the best of both. I know there is nothing inherently wrong with conservatives or liberals or fundamentalists or radicals. I know, because of my own family history, we can get along, and we can respect each other. I also know that our personalities and outlooks determine partly why we choose one party, or one approach to problem-solving, over another.

I have had, perhaps, a more ecumenical, and also a better experience with religion and with people of other political parties than many. I have met the best Christians of all types—from the most fundamentalist to the most liberal. I have found that none of them are so easily categorized. I have observed great faith and compassionate service from many people who are motivated by their faith and by their love of Christ.

In my discussions with Christians, I have always been amazed at how accepting and loving most are. I have found tolerance among the fundamentalists, and a commitment to Christ and the Bible in those considered liberal. My experiences have consistently moved me beyond stereotypes.

This is not to say there aren't differences among Christians, but I do believe labels aren't quite as neat as we like to make them. And until recently, I found that many of us could coexist as those who love Christ.

But something changed during these last few years. I noticed that the preaching from pulpits, the political ads, and the news from the television and newspapers expressed the view that somehow the Republicans owned God.

I began to feel that some Republicans actually believed that "Christian Democrat" was an oxymoron. When I attended evangelical churches, I felt insulted and offended by their negative comments about anyone who wasn't a Republican when I know, as do many Republicans, that Jimmy Carter, Al Gore, Bill Clinton, and John Kerry are all devout Christians.

What happened to our country? Instead of religion pulling us together to create a more just and loving society, it created malice, and even hatred, as if we Christians had become a dysfunctional family—unforgiving, and unaccepting of anyone who does not express themselves exactly as we do. It often seemed as if each Christian foot, hand, arm, demanded we be exactly like them. We had become dismembered, disembodied, incapable of moving together toward the society we kept insisting we wanted.

Instead of bringing about less judgment and more listening, we became blind to each other, and less respectful. Instead of working together to build a more just and loving society that acts in line with our Christian values, we built a less merciful and less compassionate society. Instead of bringing about a more peaceful and harmonious world, we brought about more dissension.

Non-Christians often told me they saw Christians as vicious, vitriolic, and at war with each other, like brothers and sisters having childish spats. How and when had we become so un-Christlike?

As a Christian who is also a writer, I realized I had to make a choice: either withdraw from the political scene for my peace of mind, or work to clarify my vision of how religion and politics can best work together. My spiritual journey for the last thirty-five years has been toward being a bridge-builder and a unifier. And yet, when asked to write this book, I realized I was taking on an intrinsically divisive topic—politics and religion. After much prayer, meditation, and discussion, I decided I was not only willing to do this, but desired to address an issue that needs to be resolved among Christians.

By no means do I believe that Democrats have some exclusive claim on God. To believe this would simply be adding more fuel to the fire. But it is time for Democrats to give an accounting of how Christian values are expressed through the Democratic Party. As Christians and as Democrats, we too are voting our values. We have a reason for our choices.

For those of you reading this book who are Republicans, I hope that it brings you new respect and understanding for your fellow Christians. For those of you who are Democrats, I hope that it helps you to articulate your values without feeling defensive or judgmental of others. This book may also speak to non-Christians; people of many faiths share the same commitment to mercy, compassion, unity, and peace. Many of us want to bring our values into the political arena. Virtually every religion includes a golden rule to guide our behavior. Most Christian values are universal values, and can, and should, provide a guide for moral and spiritual policies.

For those readers who are unsure about which party and which policies best express your values, perhaps this book will bring you to some new decisions about who you are, what you believe as a citizen of our country and of our world, and what actions you can take to help create a better world for us all.

Chapter One

How Would Jesus Vote?

*"[You] have neglected the weightier matters
of the Law—justice, mercy, good faith!"*

MATTHEW 23:23

Jesus and the prophets shared a vision for a people and a nation—that a nation would respond to its people with justice and mercy and good faith. These Christian values are also democratic values, asking us to come together to create a free, equal, and kind society that cares for all its citizens. As Christians, we are asked to help remove structures that oppress its citizens. Christian values recognize the redemptive potential and possibilities of humanity. Democracy provides a voice for the majority as well as the minority and promises freedom and protection for all. A democratic nation, founded on religious principles, struggles to create unity out of diversity, without compromising either one.

But how do we get there? In the vice-presidential debates in 2004, Dick Cheney was asked how his administration would bridge the divide to bring unity to the country. He said, "I believe it is essential for us to do everything we can to garner as much support from the other side of the aisle as possible . . . there are some Democrats who agree with our approach." For Mr. Cheney, unity meant the other side would agree with him.

If our country is dependent upon a one-party system, in which everyone thinks and believes and acts the same, we have no hope as a nation, for we will never find unity that way. We cannot, and will not, achieve unity if we continue to go about it as we have in the last few years. There have been many voices calling us to be a Christian nation, governed by Christian values with a Christian government; yet, in spite of all the Christians in government, we have not become a kinder and more just nation. Like the early Christians so often scolded by Paul for their divisiveness, we have failed to become a united people.

A House Divided Cannot Stand

We live in a divided nation. This is not just a division of Democrats versus Republicans. This is a division of Christians versus everybody else and Christians versus other Christians. The conservative Christians wonder if the more liberal Christians take the Bible seriously enough; they are concerned that the country will go to the dogs if the liberals get back in power, fearing that all of our values will be lost and that there will be rampant abortions and millions more homosexuals in our society. The liberal Christians fear that the conservatives will take away our democratic rights. They don't like the judgmental attitude of some of the more conservative Christians and are concerned that the conservatives don't care about important Christian issues such as poverty, war, ecology, and civil rights. Even though we profess the same faith, read the same Holy Bible, and try to be good followers of Christ, both sides, deep down, wonder if the other side is "suitably" Christian.

Why is it that the same Christians who are helpful, kind, and supportive of each other individually can be so vicious and vindictive when they enter into the social and political sphere?

I know many Christians, and am friends with a wide variety of Christians, who would call themselves fundamentalists, conservatives, Evangelicals, mainstream Christians, or liberal. (For a discussion of the different groups found within Christianity in this country, see the Appendix, "Christian Values and Christian Viewpoints.") On the personal level, I know I can call on any one of them if I'm in trouble. They are supportive of me, pray for me and for my friends and relatives who are sick, wish me well, and exemplify the love of Christ in their lives.

Yet, when I turn on the television, read the newspapers, read books written by some Christians, I find a level of nastiness, revenge, and downright hatred that astonishes me. My non-Christian friends have often told me they could never even consider exploring Christianity because of its public face. For them, Christianity means self-righteousness, pride, intolerance, and mean-spiritedness. And I must agree with their perception. If I weren't a Christian, and had to decide whether I would become one based on what I see from Christians who are the extreme public face of our religion, I'm not sure I could find my way to Christ. The vicious extremists, who seem to represent

Christianity because they have the loudest and most confident voices, have taken the love, kindness, compassion, and mercy out of Christianity and sounded their views with a passionate self-righteous fervor and vindictiveness that smack more of witch-hunting than of the egalitarian, embracing ideals that Jesus taught.

All of us Christians, whether conservative or liberal, have not done enough to denounce this viewpoint and let the world know this is not the face of Christ. Rather than banding together, we have divided and separated. We have allowed our faith to be distorted and misinterpreted. We would rather claim allegiance to a political party than to our faith.

This attitude has not only made us divided among ourselves, but divided from others around the world. The truth is, many people hate us. I have found, in my travels abroad, that most people don't hate individual Americans, but they no longer understand the attitudes of our country. They see Americans, collectively, as hateful, intolerant, and noncooperative with the world community. They see us as bullies in the world and condescending in our attitudes toward others. They see us as impossible to work with, with no respect for others, and little respect for each other. Many abroad are astounded by what our country has become. They don't understand our rhetoric about Christian values, because what they see doesn't strike them as values, or Christian at all. We have turned away from a gospel of love and a gospel of Christ in our politics, and have turned toward judgment, malice, and pride.

What is happening to us as Christians? Why do we keep attacking each other and demonizing each other, as if one party is the Great Satan that will bring down civilization and the other owns the Immaculate Heart of Jesus? Although Christians from both parties feel under attack, and both parties have attacked back, as a Christian Democrat I am appalled, puzzled, and offended by the constant attacks from Republican Christians, which come in the name of Jesus.[1]

A number of Republican Party spokesmen—including James Dobson from Focus on the Family; Senator Bill Frist; Representative Tom DeLay; and Tony Perkins, President of the Family Research Council—have said, in many different ways, that Democrats are "'God's people' haters,"[2] that they are enemies of Christianity, and that Democrats attack people of faith. Perkins has said the Democrats are working "like thieves in the night, to rob us of our Christian heritage and our religious freedoms."[3]

To say this, they have to ignore the Christian faith of most of the Democratic members of the Senate and the House. Are Patrick Leahy, John Kerry, Edward Kennedy, or Joseph Biden un-Christian, because they're Catholic? Is Hillary Clinton less Christian than Pat Roberts, even though both are Methodist? Would they tell us that President Carter wasn't Baptist enough? Would they reject Bill Clinton even though he was Southern Baptist, saying he didn't pass their litmus test? At what point do we decide, as Christians, that this kind of judgment about each other's souls is both un-Christian and un-American?

Protestant theologian C. S. Lewis said, "Democracy demands that little men should not take big ones too seriously; it dies when it is full of little men who think they are big themselves."[4] Perhaps it is time we denounce much of this rhetoric, for the sake of democracy, rather than embracing the walls that separate us.

We have become so divided that it seems issues no longer matter; all that's of importance is the party in which they're cloaked. Do we honestly believe this is how we create a good, just, and compassionate nation? When Christians start disdaining other Christians, there is no hope of working together toward a better society. Christians ask for a Christian nation, but now that we have a nation governed mainly by Christians, we find that instead of enjoying the fruits of the spirit and a more compassionate and effective society, we have, instead, become more divided than ever. Are we so out of sorts with each other that we honestly believe there is no way we can work together from across the political divide?

What we see is politicians using Christianity to manipulate their own agenda rather than using Christian values to guide our nation.

As a Christian who is also a Democrat, I have never felt hated by other Christians—until recently. The last three Evangelical churches I attended preached politics from the pulpit and made it very clear that Christians were expected to vote, or to have voted, for Republicans. I was offended by such an attitude and wondered why they didn't put a sign in the front that said, "Democrats are not welcome here!"

I have heard statements that vilify the Democrats, while praising George W. Bush with words that verge on worship and sometimes even idolatry.[5] I have heard prayers that thank God, fervently, that we have Mr. Bush in the White House, and that we now have this small window of four more years to "fix" everything, before the demonic Democrats have the chance of taking power away again.[6]

In Galatians 5, Paul says, "The whole of the Law is summarized in the one commandment: you must love your neighbor as yourself. If you go snapping at one another and tearing one another to pieces, take care: you will be eaten up by one another." Paul lists the problems when Spirit is not at work: "antagonisms, rivalry, jealousy, bad temper and quarrels, disagreements, factions and malice"—all the traits we read about almost daily in our newspapers and see daily on our television sets.

We have forgotten how to serve the Truth, the Just, the Good, and only gnaw at each other's belief systems and behavior. Is the Holy Spirit truly present in this behavior?

Which Is the Christian Political Party?

Both the Republican and Democratic parties and some of the others as well are made up of millions of Christians.

In the 2004 presidential election, many Republicans believed they knew exactly how Jesus would have voted—Republican. The Republican vote was called the "values vote." But the statistics and the actions tell us otherwise. Although the press implied that George W. Bush got the Christian vote, this is not true.

Although Mr. Bush received 78 percent of the Evangelical votes, that still left more than one out of five Christian Evangelicals who voted otherwise. The foremost evangelist of our time—Billy Graham—is a Democrat. Catholics, and other Protestants, on the whole, were almost equally divided between George W. Bush, who is a Methodist, and John Kerry, who is a Catholic.[7]

Even the breakdown of voters is not so neat. Some liberals voted for Mr. Bush; some conservatives for Mr. Kerry. Some people who are pro-choice voted Republican. Some who are anti-abortion voted for Kerry. Many who voted Republican confess to agonizing over their decision and finally voting for Mr. Bush because we were in the middle of a war and they felt we should stay with the same leader. Some of these have told me they now regret their vote.

Clearly, millions of Christians in both parties voted their values and their priorities.

Beyond Party to People

If we move beyond party to people, a Christian Democrat and a Christian Republican might agree on many issues. Sometimes they vote according to whom they feel they can best trust to keep promises. They vote for the person who seems to have the same priorities as they do, or the one they think can best exemplify these values in our government. Many vote for the issues, while trying to assess the character of the candidate.

Both democracy and Christianity are challenging. They challenge us to go against our seemingly natural human behaviors of hatred, intolerance, and self-righteousness and move toward an affirmation of equality. They ask us to find unity in a nation made up of diverse peoples.

On the surface, there do seem to be issues that are not easily resolved, because there seems to be an inner contradiction between Christianity and democracy. Churches often ask us to be homogeneous in our beliefs and actions. Churches have creeds, and dogmas, and statements of belief, and the members are asked to, at least verbally, agree with them. But our country is not homogeneous. From the beginning, settlers of our country came to America to find freedom, and soon found that there was a diverse group of others, all of whom wanted the same freedom for themselves. Early on, many of the early settlers decided they may as well respect that and create a democratic system.

All of us are constantly in a struggle between the desire to be inclusive and the desire to be exclusive. We are always being pushed between our natural suspicion of each other and the command to love our neighbor, even when the neighbor is someone far away, or someone we really don't like at all.

I have heard time and again that we are a Christian nation. But we are not a Christian nation—either in many of our actions or in the makeup of our citizens. No matter how much we might like to be homogeneous in religion, we are not. We are a diverse nation, made up of Christians, Jews, Buddhists, Muslims, Hindus, Wiccans, Hare Krishnas, Sikhs, New Agers, atheists, agnostics, and a few Zoroaster followers, among others.

There are many people other than Christians who have values. Many of those values are similar to ours—among them, the values of freedom, equality, honesty, justice, mercy, compassion, and the golden rule. Many people besides Christians see America as the land of opportunity, the land where they can achieve their dreams. Although there may be more of "us" than "them," and although our country may have been founded mainly (but not entirely) by Christians, our country has strived from the very beginning to give freedom and justice to all. As

Christians living in a democratic nation, we have to remember
that what we desire for ourselves must be available for all. Sup-
pressing another's freedom is not the answer.

I have heard that everything would be fine if we just followed
Christ. Of course, if we all were more Christlike, things would
be much better. We would see the fruits of the Spirit all around
us—love, joy, peace, patience, kindness, goodness, faithfulness,
gentleness, and self-control.[8] But we're not as Christlike as we
would think. Unfortunately, our sinful and flawed and imperfect
nature keeps getting in the way.

Was Jesus Political?

On the surface, it might seem as if Jesus was not a political person but was someone who focused, instead, on individuals and
individual relationships. He certainly did not live up to the Jewish hopes for a political Messiah. The Jews in Jesus' day imag-
ined a militant Messiah who would lead an army, overthrow the
oppressive rule of Rome, and establish a religious kingdom.

We can, however, see some of the political viewpoints of
Jesus through the actions he took and those he didn't take. Jesus
didn't identify with any of the political structures of the day. He
rejected the Sadducees, the conservatives who were willing to
go along with foreign domination provided it didn't compro-
mise their position. He confronted the Pharisees, who observed
religious practices in great detail, made hundreds of oppressive religious laws, and also supported the established powers
of the day. He never joined the Essenes, who rejected political

involvement and took no part in any of the religious ceremonies because they considered them impure. They formed a separate sect, and moved to Qumran by the Dead Sea. He was not part of the Zealots, one of the most politically active groups. They were nationalists, who wanted a radical transformation of existing political institutions through violent revolution.

Many of Jesus' followers were from different political parties with different political and religious beliefs. Simon, called the Zealot, would have either been a revolutionary or a sympathizer with the group that desired to overthrow the Roman government. Matthew, the tax collector, worked for the oppressive government that Simon wanted to overthrow. Yet, there's no evidence that Jesus tried to change their political parties, or even their religion. He wanted to change their hearts and their actions.[9]

Was Jesus Conservative or Liberal?

The labels of conservative and liberal have been so overused they have become almost meaningless. One side hates the other side, even though those considered to be liberals often hold conservative values, and those considered to be conservative often hold liberal values.

The word "conservative" comes from the word "conserve," which can mean "to preserve." Generally, conservatives want to preserve the status quo. They prefer to maintain existing habits and views and institutions. A true conservative usually wants government to have a limited role in social and economic

affairs. At their best, conservatives ground our country by recognizing the ideals of the past and giving us a solid foundation
on which to stand.

At their worst, conservatives can be inflexible, rigid, legal-
istic, and immovable. They are sometimes fearful of risks and
distrustful of change. Because they are often unable to imagine
other possibilities or to believe that change can lead us to a better society, conservatives are less apt to envision new ways to
solve social problems.

Liberal is a word coming from the Latin *liberare*—to set
free or to liberate. Liberals tend to advocate reforms that would
achieve greater freedom for citizens. To achieve that, they are
more apt to criticize the status quo, imagine new possibilities,
and ask how it can be done better. They are willing to be uncon-
ventional and untraditional in order to solve a problem.

At their best, they tend to be tolerant of others and want
to remove restraints to the freedom of all citizens, not just for
themselves. They are progressive, wanting to improve the social
welfare of others. The word "liberal" often means generous and
bounteous and open-handed, as used when someone gives liberally to charity. At their most extreme, liberals can become so
freedom-minded that their actions lead to excess, anarchy, and
a lack of restraint that can become destructive.

Both of these positions need to be more balanced. Lacking balance, either position can lead to the vicious extremism
that we see in almost all political parties and religions—rang-
ing from the fundamentalists who will kill in the name of their
party or their religion, to the radicals who destroy property and
create anarchy in the name of freedom.

Like most of us, Jesus exemplified both conservative and liberal values. There were certain values he wanted to conserve; there were others that he wanted to liberate from a rule-oriented culture in order to reinterpret, broaden, or change them.

The Freedom to Love God

The most important value that Jesus wanted to conserve was the commandment to love the Lord your God with all your heart, with all your soul, with all your mind, and all your strength.[10] Love of God is above all things and is the guiding principle throughout the entire Bible. How to love God has been one of the thorniest issues our country has ever confronted.

Our nation was founded by many who loved God. Before the Constitution was written, the early colonies tried to legislate the love of God. They became repressive when they tried to impose laws about how this love was to be shown. The Massachusetts Bay Colony persecuted any who didn't love God in the same way they did. They banished those who didn't agree with them, particularly the Quakers. Besides banishment, Quakers were imprisoned, whipped, branded, burned, and enslaved; some had their ears cut off and their property confiscated; several were put to death for insisting on the right to worship in their own way.[11]

Puritan minister Roger Williams (who later helped found the first Baptist church in America) was banished from Boston because he believed that everyone had the right to think and worship as he pleased. In his pamphlet called *The Bloudy Tenent of Persecution, for the Cause of Conscience,* published in 1644,

Williams said, "How ghastly and unbelieved . . . was the damage done and the number of innocent human beings slaughtered in the effort to make men and women worship God in some certain way."[12] He believed in separation of church and state, so neither could control the other, and complete toleration by the government of all sorts of religion, even the religion of the Indians. Williams, the Quakers, and other tolerant Christians established freedom of worship and freedom from a state-sponsored religion.

The writers of the Constitution didn't want to legislate religion. They recognized that democracies cannot be ruled by prayer. As a result, the Constitution was designed to try to channel these motives in the direction of the public good.[13]

One of the clearest definitions between the Republican and Democratic values lies with the question of what part religion should play in a nation. The Democrats have had a fairly consistent policy to protect our religious freedoms. The Republicans have, during some previous administrations, been protective of religious freedom. However, the last few decades have seen the rise of the Moral Majority and the Religious Right within the Republican Party, which itself has become increasingly influential, potentially threatening freedom of worship.

Who Are the Dominionists and What Control Do They Want?

Within the Republican Party is an influential group of Christians called the Dominionists, who believe they are called to have dominion over the government. Their goal is to expand their political influence in the Republican Party, and therefore, throughout America. It is estimated that about 35 million Christians, almost all of them Republicans, subscribe to these theories.[14] Christian Democrats are particularly concerned about our country going backward and becoming less democratic, rather than more so, as a result of the increasing power of this group within the Republican Party.

The movement was begun by D. James Kennedy in Florida in 1959. (Kennedy also helped found the Moral Majority in 1979, along with the Rev. Jerry Falwell and others.) Kennedy says, "Our job is to reclaim America for Christ, whatever the cost. As the vice regents of God, we are to exercise godly dominion and influence over our neighborhoods, our schools, our government, our literature and arts, our sports arenas, our entertainment media, our news media, our scientific endeavors—in short, over every aspect and institution of human society." There is nothing wrong with bringing values into every aspect of our social and political life. That's what we would want in a country that tries to serve the Good. But Kennedy is not talking about trying to make Christianity more prevalent in American political policy; rather, he is promoting the sole use of the Dominionist brand of Christianity in making public policy—to the exclusion of not only other faiths, but also other interpretations of Christianity. This kind of exclusion and lack of protection for those unlike themselves is unconstitutional and unjust.

Another Dominionist, David Limbaugh, brother of Rush Limbaugh, says, "We have a right, indeed an obligation, to govern." They believe that the government's work is to proselytize, to protect property rights, and to promote homeland security but not to promote social change. They want to restore school prayer, put a Bible in each classroom, and criminalize the homosexual lifestyle. In addition, they want anyone who protests American policies to be arrested for treason.[15]

Some in this group want all citizens to pay "tithes" to church organizations, which are to become social-welfare agencies for the government. Others want the death penalty for so-called moral crimes such as blasphemy, sodomy, witchcraft, and apostasy. They are upset about a court ruling that said that executing minors was unconstitutional. The Family Research Council, which is made up of Dominionists and is one of the most influential and radical Christian Right lobbying groups, has taken a stand against teaching tolerance and diversity.[16] With the Dominionists in charge, all other voices, except a certain brand of conservative Christians, would be silenced.

What would this mean for you and me? Let's take the controversial subject of school prayer. In a state-sponsored religion, whose prayer would prevail? I can think of a number of prayers that would be counter to my own belief systems, as well as the belief systems of many others.

I can imagine a prayer from a teacher or preacher that says, "Our Lord and Commander, we ask that you give your power to the troops in Iraq and help them to overcome the enemy as we fight this great Crusade to lead us to truth."

I have heard prayers like this. To me, it's a self-righteous prayer that makes nationalism the religion, rather than Christianity. It sees the Other as the enemy, rather than as the Neighbor, and it implies that there will be hundreds, if not hundreds of thousands of the enemy killed in the name of Jesus. As a pacifist, I find no room for my own Christian belief system in this prayer.

I also can imagine another kind of prayer, which would be anathema to most conservatives, and perhaps to millions of other Christians as well: "Our Ground of all being, Mother Earth, Father Sky, embrace our bodies and bring us into unity with you."

Although this may be a more loving prayer, it is so vague and unspecific that it would be meaningless to many. Yet, I have also heard prayers such as this.

I can imagine nationalist prayers that would insist on our complete loyalty to our president, even when he is lying and covering up treasonous or illegal or immoral activities. Do we really want to be saying state-sponsored prayers that keep us from questioning Watergate? Or the Iran-Contra illegal deals? Or the prisoner abuse in Iraq, Afghanistan, and Guantánamo Bay?

What about classrooms in which most of the students are not Christian but Jewish, or Buddhist or Muslim, or not religious at all? Does the majority rule? Will we all be asked to chant? Will the non-Christians be forced to pray "in Jesus' name"?

What Else Would Be Changed?

In gathering everything in the United States under one belief system, the Dominionists would also change the courts. James

Dobson, Tony Perkins, and former House Majority Leader Tom
DeLay discussed what to do with courts that are not conservative enough: de-fund them. DeLay said in April 2005, "We set
up the courts. We can un-set the courts. We have the power of
the purse."

Perkins explained what he meant by de-funding the courts.
Instead of going through a process of impeaching judges, which
can take a long time, Congress, through the Appropriations
Committee, could just "take away the [judge's] bench, all of his
staff, and he's just sitting out there with nothing to do." Which
courts are they talking about? The courts that are not conservative enough for them—such as the Ninth Circuit Court of
California. As Dobson explained, "Very few people know this,
that the Congress can simply disenfranchise a court . . . They
don't have to fire anybody or impeach them or go through that
battle. All they have to do is say the 9th Circuit doesn't exist
anymore, and it's gone." Dobson claimed they had the right to
do this, because the GOP won the election. "We've got a right
to hold them accountable for what happens here." But winning
an election does not give anyone a mandate to tread on the
rights of the minority.

The Dominionists are against any voice for the Democrats
or for other Christians. But they're also against what they call
"squishy" and "weak" Republican senators who are not always
in agreement with them. This includes Republican moderates
such as Senators Olympia J. Snowe, Susan Collins, Lincoln
Chafee, Arlen Specter, Chuck Hagel, Mitch McConnell, and
George Allen, all of whom the Dominionists felt needed to be
shaken up. Dobson was personally affronted that they didn't

follow everything he said: "Sometimes it's just amazing to me that they [these senators] seem to forget how they got here."[17]

The Dominionists seem to forget about our democratic rights to free elections, the protection of the minority, and the right to diverse voices in government. They deny and defy the Founding Fathers' system of checks and balances, wherein the executive, the legislative, and the judicial branches of government are kept in integration and balance so that none obtains overwhelming power or influence over the others. They apparently see the executive branch as a ruler and want to be sure the other two branches fall in line or are paralyzed. Our government was set up to guard us against the power of a group such as this. Even though this group lays claim to democratic and Christian values, it practices neither.

George W. Bush sought the blessing of the Dominionists before running for president, and he continues to consult them on matters of federal policy, in some cases on an ongoing basis. Pastor Ted Haggard, head of the National Association of Evangelicals, speaks weekly to President Bush or to one of his advisers, as does Rev. Richard Land, the top lobbyist for the Southern Baptist Convention.

The Dominionists' troubling vision for our country is not shared by all conservative Christians. Some are embarrassed and dismayed by this group's views. Many conservative and fundamentalist Christians, as well as mainstream and liberal Christians, are not comfortable with this extreme theocratic vision for our country or with this expression of our faith.

Luis Palau, an evangelical preacher who is close to Billy Graham, bristles at the coarseness of these calls for absolute power.

Palau is concerned about the ways this influential Republican Christian group belittles homosexuals, "effete" intellectuals, and secular humanists. Palau says, "If we become called to Christ, we will build an effective nation through personal ethics. When you lead a life of purity, when you respect your wife and are good to your family, when you don't waste money gambling and womanizing, you begin to work for better schools, for more protection and safety from your community. All change, historically, comes from the bottom up."[18]

Other evangelical Christians are equally concerned about this movement. Senator Mark Pryor, an evangelical Christian, says, "It is presumptuous of them [the Christian Right] to think they represent all Christians in America, even to say they represent all evangelical Christians."[19]

As Christians, we have to come to terms with what kind of government we want. Personally, I don't want it run by the flawed and imperfect theology of the Dominionists, any more than I want to run the nation with my own flawed and imperfect theology. I know, for sure, that I don't have a handle on God, or a corner on knowing the perfect will of God. I know, without a doubt, that some of my interpretations of Bible verses may not be considered accurate. I am absolutely convinced that God is far bigger than anything my limited mind can contain and that I am far from showing the perfect love Jesus has commanded us to show each other. I also know, with certainty, that the Dominionists are no different. Like all of us, they are sinners and flawed. Do we want them running our country? If not them, then whom can we trust? Neither the Dominionists, nor the conservatives, nor the liberals, nor the humanists. We should trust the voice of the people.

C.S. Lewis, the Protestant writer and theologian, said he believed in democracy "because I believe in the Fall of Man. I think most people [want democracy] for the opposite reason. A great deal of democratic enthusiasm descends from the ideas of people . . . who believed in democracy because they thought mankind so wise and good that everyone deserved a share in the government. The danger of defending democracy on those grounds is that they're not true . . . I find that they're not true without looking further than myself. I don't deserve a share in governing a hen-roost, much less a nation. Nor do most people . . . The real reason for democracy is . . . Mankind is so fallen that no man can be trusted with unchecked power over his fellows. Aristotle said that some people were only fit to be slaves. I do not contradict him. But I reject slavery because I see no men fit to be masters."[20]

Some might think that a sort of theocratic rule is fine, since those governing are religious. But Thomas Jefferson believed that our nation would encounter the same problem if one group of people determined the religion of another group. He said, "Difference of opinion is advantageous in religion. The several sects perform the office of a censor . . . over such other. Is uniformity attainable? Millions of innocent men, women and children, since the introduction of Christianity have been burnt, tortured, fined, imprisoned; yet we have not advanced one inch toward uniformity. What has been the effect of coercion? To make one half of the world fools and the other half hypocrites."[21] This conservative value of religion and love of God only works when it is liberally given to all its citizens and each can freely choose how to exercise it.

Upholding True Conservative Values

Another value that Jesus affirmed is the value of accountability and responsibility. Leaders are to rule justly, not be beholden to the rich, the powerful, the influential.[22]

Both political parties have had a number of presidents, and members of Congress, who have lied, deceived, and tried to get away with breaking laws. It is a right and righteous act to hold these people accountable. Yet, the scandals of the Republican Party since 2000 have often involved those who demand accountability from others, but not for themselves. When House Majority Leader Tom DeLay was first being investigated for breaking various ethical laws, the Republicans tried to change the ethics rules to protect him, until an outcry forced them to stop. When he was indicted on several counts, including breaking laws that carried a prison sentence, the Republicans blamed the Democrats for making ethical breaches a political issue. Instead of truth-telling, blaming became the focus of the discussions.

The value of holding each person accountable for his or her actions, as taught by Jesus and the prophets, is a conservative value. Justice transcends political parties.

The Bible also begins with a commandment that none of the prophets, or Jesus or Paul, have overturned—the commandment to tend the environment that God has given us. Although this is a conservative value, it has been adopted by those considered liberals. We are asked to conserve, preserve, and care for the world that God has given to us. Noah went to considerable trouble, under God's command, to make sure that the animals didn't become extinct. Jesus extols the beauty of the lilies of the field and the birds of the air, telling us that God will care for us, as He cares for nature. If there is one Christian value that should transcend political parties, it should be our care for the environment.

Fiscal Responsibility

Fiscal responsibility is usually considered a conservative value, although the Democratic Party has been more fiscally responsible than the Republican Party for more than twenty-five years.

There is a great deal said about money in the Bible—much of it about giving money to the poor and about letting our money work for us.[23] Our country rarely follows these values—spending more than it has, not caring enough for the needy, only rarely creating surpluses.

We love money. It defines us as powerful and comfortable and important. We use it to gain political favor and to increase our clout. We spend it easily. We deny it to some, give a great deal of it to others. We hide and waste a great deal of it.

Jesus tells a story about the boss who gave money to his various servants and went away for a week. When he returned, he was pleased with the servants who used the money to increase the master's wealth. He punished the servant who hid the money and did nothing with it. Jesus told the story of the prodigal son, who was wasteful with his money. Although he was forgiven and accepted back into the family, misusing his inheritance led to great misery.[24]

Have we been good stewards? The Republican Party used to be considered the party of fiscal responsibility, but this has not been true since Ronald Reagan's presidency. President Reagan ran up the national debt to historic proportions, followed by President George H.W. Bush and now George W. Bush.

When Bill Clinton entered office, there was a budget deficit of about $250 billion, which he inherited from the spending practices of both Mr. Reagan and George H.W. Bush. When Clinton left office, he had turned this deficit around, and left George W. Bush with a budget surplus of around $523 billion.[25] According to House Minority Whip Steny Hoyer, over a ten-year period, this was a projected surplus of $5.6 trillion.[26]

This did not last long. George W. Bush has run up the largest debt in American history. By 2003, Mr. Bush had run up a budget deficit of $378 billion. The 2005 budget deficit is expected to exceed $427 billion.

What is the consequence of this deficit? David Walker, the comptroller general of the General Accounting Office, says that without reform, the economy could slowly grind to a halt. "We could be doing nothing more than paying interest on federal debt in 2040 if we don't end up engaging in some fundamental reforms of entitlement programs, mandatory spending, discretionary spending and tax policy."[27]

Some of this debt comes from mismanagement and from a lack of foresight to prevent or to better deal with catastrophes. In the cases of Iraq and the damage from Hurricane Katrina and Hurricane Rita, warnings that would have prevented tragedy were ignored. The U.S. government was warned by both the U.S. Army Corps of Engineers and the Southeast Louisiana Urban Flood Control Project that the levees would break if there were a category 4 or 5 hurricane. They asked for some millions of dollars to repair them, which was denied. The levees did break, and now it's costing billions.

Although George W. Bush had been warned about the problems that would ensue if he went into Iraq without a well-thought-out plan for rebuilding the country, he went in anyway, without the plan. In spite of billions of dollars put into the country, much of the money goes for security, and for repairing, and repairing again, what continues to be blown up by insurgents.

When we had a surplus, Mr. Bush refunded money, including large amounts to the people who least needed it—the upper middle class and the rich. Although repealing the tax cut for the very rich would help matters a great deal, Mr. Bush has refused to do so.

The Liberal Values of Jesus

Although both the Republican and Democratic Parties contain conservatives and liberals, the Republican Party has increasingly sided with its more conservative members. The Republican Party has made "liberal" a dirty word.

Yet, our country was founded on liberal and liberating values. The Founding Fathers were willing to change the status

quo, overthrow an oppressive government, and create a new
form of government by the people, of the people, for the people.
Many Christians in the early years of our country's history questioned the laws of the time, and changed them, in order to create a freer, more just society.

All men are created equal under God, but in the period of
time leading up to 1860, they were born into an unequal system. Only white men who owned property enjoyed inalienable
rights. Blacks were considered three-fifths of a person. Married
women had almost no civil rights at all. Many Christians, but
not all, supported this idea, quoting the Bible to justify slavery
and oppression of women. Many Christians limited and resisted
extending equal rights to others.

How did this change? Through the work of other Christians.
Most of the first abolitionists were Christians—mainly Quakers,
Methodists, and Congregationalists. Over time, the impulse to
liberate women grew also from Christian roots.

The most recent and extraordinary example of this process
was the civil rights movement in the twentieth century, led by
a Baptist minister, Dr. Martin Luther King Jr. The movement
was conceived in African-American churches and sustained by
Christians of all racial and ethnic groups. Many Christians have
been, and continue to be, at the forefront of the fight for the
civil rights of others.

Throughout the Gospels, we see the portrait of Jesus as a
man who questioned the prevailing religious and social establishment. Many actions that Jesus took, and stories that he
told, were about liberating people from legal, religious, and

governmental oppression. Rather than demanding adherence to religious dogmas and the hundreds of religious laws, he questioned the way things were, and followed the freer Law of Love.

Jesus transcended sexism when he talked to a woman at the well in Samaria.[28] He affirmed Mary's desire to listen and to learn, rather than Martha's playing of the traditional woman's role.[29] Women followed him around the countryside and he accepted them, even though this would have been against the social customs of his age. Women became some of his most beloved followers, and some of the leaders in the early Church.[30]

He challenged the racism of his day by telling a story about a man he perceived as good and righteous—a Samaritan, one of the most hated people.[31] This would be similar to telling a Klansman a story about a good and righteous African-American.

He challenged classism, by associating with the lowlifes of society—the rejects, the prostitutes, the tax collectors, the outcasts, the sick, the lepers, and the untouchables, even eating with them and saying that they would enter the kingdom before the religious leaders of the day.[32] He pardoned the repentant thief on the cross, telling him that he would join Jesus in Paradise.[33]

The Democrats have had a long history of backing equal rights and overcoming unequal laws. It was a Democratic president—Lyndon B. Johnson—who signed civil rights legislation to bring equal rights to ethnic minorities. The Democrats, to the chagrin of many Republicans, have been consistent in their desire to see equal rights for all people—women, ethnic minorities, those of other religions, and those of different sexual orientation.

The Democratic Party Platform for 2004 begins by offering its vision of America—"an America that offers opportunity, rewards responsibility, and rejoices in diversity . . . We will honor the values of a strong American community: widening the circle of equality, protecting the sanctity of freedom, and deepening our commitment to this country. We recommit to the ideal of a people united in helping one another, an ideal as old as the faiths we follow and as great as the country we love."

Liberating the Law

Jesus, as well as Paul, brought liberal values to the idea of marriage. A Jewish man and woman were supposed to marry and to have children. Jesus was single, and didn't fulfill the appropriate social and religious customs of his age. Paul clarified that it didn't matter if a person were single or married; each was to be valued.[34]

Jesus was against capital punishment, a position that is considered a liberal value. He forgave the woman caught in the act of adultery, and freed her, even though the religious law of his time proclaimed that she be stoned to death.[35]

Jesus rethought the idea of forgiveness, clarifying that no longer should one seek revenge through an "eye for an eye"; nor should one forgive another only seven times, but rather seventy times seven.[36]

In many ways, Jesus was far more radical than are the most liberal members of Congress, asking us to act in a way that we often find impossible and impractical.

He changed the way we were to think about the enemy. We are to make friends with our enemies, recognizing that to not do this would cause nothing but trouble.[37] Jesus expanded our idea of the neighbor, telling us that we are to think of our enemy as our neighbor, and he added a new commandment: to love our neighbor as ourselves. This doesn't mean that we are naive about evil, but that we don't add fuel to the fires of hatred. Rather than demonizing and attacking the enemy, we should use diplomacy, which is far more in line with the values of Jesus.[38]

Jesus practiced nonviolent resistance to oppressive laws. He suggested that we love our enemies—feed them, clothe them, care for them, and "offer no resistance to the wicked." This turns the enemy into a friend. He also suggested a subversive tactic that is often used in nonviolent resistance. If the person of his day were asked for his coat, he was to give the cloak as well. If he were asked to go one mile, he was to go two miles.[39]

Why is this nonviolent resistance? If a person in Biblical times gave up his coat and cloak, he would be naked, thereby shaming the person who asked him. It wouldn't take long for the Romans to decide that this was embarrassing and not effective.

A Roman was allowed to ask his subject to carry a burden for one mile, but not for longer. If someone started to walk the second mile, the Roman would be breaking the law. It wouldn't take long for the Romans to stop asking, once they realized that they couldn't stop their subjects from walking that second mile.

Overturning the Social Structures

Jesus and the prophets rethought the social structures that generally rewarded the rich and powerful and asked us to change our focus to the poor and the needy. The prophets asked for a compassionate nation, and Jesus asked for a compassionate people. Who do we particularly need to care about? Those people who cannot give back to us, but who are in need of our care.

Jesus challenged us to give respect, care, and our help to others, even those unlike ourselves, and even those we might hate. How has our country responded? Racism, sexism, and ageism have continued to be ingrained in our national laws and our national identity. Any challenge to these policies is met with resistance. Republican policies have continued to resist affirmative action policies to help those who have been left out and left behind.

Jesus asks us to be fair in our dealing with others. How have we responded? Over and over again, our government has rewarded graft, corruption, and dishonesty. No-bid contracts have been given to the powerful—those close to the Bush and Cheney families—to rebuild Iraq. When these companies, such as Halliburton and Bechtel, were brought before congressional investigation committees to explain their overbilling, overcharges, and lack of effectiveness, Mr. Bush continued to reward them by giving them another contract—to help rebuild New Orleans. Whose money is being misspent? Yours and mine.

Jesus rode a donkey, not an elephant. Elephants were ridden by the rich ruling classes. Jesus didn't identify with the rich ruling classes, but with the people. He was with the people and for the people and of the people—a core value of both democracy and Christianity.

The Ethics of Jesus

Jesus asked us to go beyond the letter of the law to the spirit of the law. Christian values go beyond simple rules to difficult ethical questions.

When Jesus picked corn on the Sabbath, and healed on the Sabbath, the letter of the law said this was wrong.[40] Jesus raised the ethical question—"Does this benefit or harm others?" If it benefits others, we may need to change the law.

Our country has many difficult ethical problems to consider. Does stem cell research hurt or harm? Is it better to use stem cells to save lives, considering that the cells will be thrown away and wasted otherwise? How are we to handle the ethical dilemma of abortion, knowing that without Roe v. Wade, some women will continue to have abortions, the difference being that the rich will have safe abortions and the poor will have unsafe abortions? How are we to handle terrorism and the proliferation of nuclear weapons? And what about the wide-ranging effects of a global economy? What should we do about climate change and health care and education? The Bible gives us no clear guides on many issues, except to be willing to confront ethical problems, guided by the Holy Spirit and the Law of Love.

Vote the Golden Rule

Why do so many Christians vote Democratic? Because they see their values best expressed in the Democratic Party and they see that many of the actions and policies of Jesus are at the center of Democratic policy.

Many of us bring together our practice of religion and democracy by voting the Golden Rule. What we want for ourselves, we are also willing to give to others. We vote for the rights of others that we would also want for ourselves. We give the same protections, care, and respect to others that we would want for ourselves. For this reason, we care about the Others' rights with the same passion that we care about our own.

What would Jesus be doing in our society? As the Prince of Peace, he would be questioning our wars, which kill tens of thousands of civilians and leave tens of thousands of children homeless and as orphans.

As the One who accepts and loves, he would be rebuilding homes, instead of blowing up abortion clinics in the name of God. He'd be caring for AIDS victims instead of limiting the rights of homosexuals. He'd be volunteering at soup kitchens rather than granting tax cuts to the rich. He'd be planting trees instead of strip-mining national parks. He'd be working to take care of those who have trouble surviving in our society, rather than rewarding the rich.

He would continue to question authority, knowing that power and privilege can easily corrupt. We are told by Republicans that we must not critique our government, must not question the actions of George W. Bush. If we do, we are unpatriotic and un-American. Yet Jesus consistently questioned, critiqued, and denounced the establishment of his day. He recognized the potential that power had to become oppressive.

Jesus went beyond labels to people, beyond party to people.

Democracy asks us to debate and discuss issues to find the best solutions. It asks many of the same questions that Christianity asks:

What are the most important issues the government needs to address?

What is the goal of a Good Society?

What are the means to reach this goal?

How do we bring justice and mercy into a society, and create a society in which all of us, together, work for the Good?

Chapter Two

The Poor, the Needy,
Widows, and Orphans

*"The spirit of the Lord is on me, for he has anointed me to
bring the good news to the afflicted. He has sent me to proclaim
liberty to captives, sight to the blind, to let the oppressed go
free, to proclaim a year of favour from the Lord."*

LUKE 4:18–19

T his was Jesus' first mission statement. It is often called the
Social Gospel, because it proclaims his intent to move
people from captivity and oppression to freedom. This is not
only spiritual freedom, but proclaiming the Kingdom of God
among us, within the society in which we live, and throughout
the earth.

When Jesus quoted from Isaiah in this passage, he left out
the last phrase of the second sentence—"and a day of vengeance
for our God."[1] He put the emphasis back on the people we are
supposed to care about. This is a challenging message. Many of

us in America do not know people who are poor or destitute. If we do, we might believe their problems are of their own making and God really does help those who help themselves. Many Americans have lived in such privilege we turn our eyes away from the homeless, blame the AIDS victims for their disease, try to justify why the poor are so poor, and claim God's blessing to explain why we're so comfortable.

Our country is powerful and rich. We easily envy power and wealth, and try to get it for ourselves, forgetting that Jesus and the prophets ask us to change our perspective, and to take the side of the poor—to care about those without means, those who need healing.

The Command for Compassion

There is much disagreement about exactly what we, as Christians, should be changing in our nation. The Bible tell us nothing about many of the issues that confront us in contemporary society— whether we should talk to or negotiate with terrorists, whether our country should honor living wills, what kind of health care or educational system we should have. But there is one area in which the Bible is absolutely clear—we are to help the poor, the needy, the broken-hearted, the oppressed. The entire Bible, beginning with the stories in Genesis and throughout the Hebrew Scriptures and the New Testament, testifies that those who oppress the poor and the needy are not in God's good graces.

In Isaiah, God says "Shame on you . . . you who make unjust laws and publish burdensome decrees, depriving the poor of

justice, robbing the weakest of my people of their rights, despoil-
ing the widow and plundering the orphan."[2] God promised that
he would bring justice to them and that He would crush their
oppressors.[3]

While protecting the poor, God warns the rich: "In prosper-
ity people lose their good sense, they become no better than
dumb animals. So they go on in their self-assurance, right up to
the end they are content with their lot."[4]

In Amos he condemns the rich "for crime after crime of
Israel I will grant them no reprieve because they sell the innocent for silver and the destitute for a pair of shoes. They grind
the heads of the poor into the earth and thrust the humble out
of their way."[5]

The Bible tells us God is a stronghold for the oppressed and
he will not desert them. He listens to the laments of the broken-
hearted. He fills the starving, and rescues those in chains and
misery from hard labor. He gives the hungry a home, where they
sow the fields, and blesses them with a bountiful harvest. God
provides a refuge for the weak and seeks justice for the poor.[6]

Throughout the Bible, the words for the "poor" are not
neutral ones, but expressions of the suffering and misery they
endure. The poor person might be *ebyon*, "the one who desires,
the beggar, the one who is lacking something and who awaits it
from another," or *dal*, the "weak one, the frail one," or *ani*, "the
bent-over one, the one laboring under a weight, the one not
in possession of his whole strength and vigor, the humiliated
one" or *anawy*, "humble before God." In the New Testament,
the word *ptokos* is used, meaning "one who does not have what
is necessary to subsist, the wretched one driven into begging."[7]

It is the duty of the rich to help the poor, and the strong to protect and bring justice to the weak.[8]

The Kings and Judges of the Hebrew Scriptures were commanded to find ways to equalize that which was unequal. They had authority over the nation, and woe to them if they only honored the rich! They were told not to cheat the poor. The poor were given the right to glean the edges of the fields for food, so they would not starve in a land of plenty. A tithe was to be collected every third year for them. The rich were not to make a profit from the poor, or charge them interest on a loan, or treat them as slaves. There were special compensations for the poor so they would not appear before God empty-handed. In the year of Jubilee, the poor could return and claim their ancestral lands; the injustices of the past would be ended and they could start anew.[9]

If God had to choose sides, whose side would He be on? The needy. The suffering. Those without means. Those who have need of a loving Savior. The expected order is turned upside down in the Bible. It is not the rich and powerful who are blessed, but the poor.

Protestant theologian Karl Barth, in his *Church Dogmatics*, says the Christian community "explicitly accepts solidarity with the least of little ones . . . with those who are in obscurity and are not seen, with those who are pushed to the margin and perhaps the very outer margin of the life of human society, with fellow-creatures who temporarily at least, and perhaps permanently, are useless and insignificant and perhaps even burdensome and destructive . . . these men are recognized to be brothers of Jesus Christ . . . and therefore the community confesses Jesus Christ

Himself as finally the hungry, thirsty, naked, homeless, sick, imprisoned man . . ."[10] As we do unto the least of these, we also do unto Christ.

If there is one command in the Bible that seems absolutely clear from beginning to end, it is to help the poor. It is the greatest litmus test we can apply to any governmental policies. If we had to choose only one issue that addresses the place where Christian values and political policy clearly come together, it wouldn't be abortion, or homosexuality, or stem cell research, or even education, protecting the environment, or employment—it would be to help the poor and the oppressed. We, as Christians, are called upon to allow the light of Christ to shine on the sadness that is at the core of the human condition, and to be part of God's redemptive work on earth.

Can We Agree on Helping the Poor?

When setting out to write this book, I had presumed that this was one issue where we could find agreement among Christians. I was wrong. Although there are more than 2,000 verses in the Bible about the need for individuals and nations to help the poor and the oppressed, there is a powerful group of conservative Republican Christians that does not believe the Bible on this issue. They believe individuals and churches are asked to help the poor, if they so desire, but not nations. They believe charitable giving should only come from those who wish to give.

I must admit I was shocked to learn this. After all, this idea is coming from conservatives and fundamentalists who say they take the Bible literally. I started to question several of my colleagues who were conservative Republican Christians about this issue in order to understand it more clearly. I promised not to use their names in this book if they would clarify this issue for me.

I was told, by one conservative Christian, "We are called to help, not to force others to help or to use our mob power to steal from those who do not want to help." Another Republican Christian said liberals believe in helping the poor in various social programs. He saw the liberal Democrats as giving far too many handouts, and the government shouldn't be in that business. In his view, conservatives believe that "the church, not the government, should be involved with helping and caring for the poor."

I e-mailed him back, asking who the church is most apt to help. Certainly they are most apt to help fellow Christians. Where does that leave the immigrant who has just received citizenship but has few resources? Or the Muslim, who lives in a poor community? What about the workers who have been hurt by the Enron or WorldCom or Adelphia scandals, left out in the cold while the CEOs have made millions of dollars? What about the drastic needs that come from communities hit by a hurricane and left with billions of dollars in damage? Or from the tsunami that has washed away hundreds of thousands of people and hundreds of communities, leaving needs far beyond what one church, or two or three, or even one denomination, can handle?

One of the Christians said we should not be forced to give money to causes that we don't believe in. He is also a pacifist, so